Conte

DRINK THIS BOOK WHILE READING YOUR MORNING COFFEE

A book of devotions written by a guy that has no business writing devotions

by Dr Chris Park

The word became flesh	?
How to Kill a Giant	?
The Cross	?

My wife tells me I'm weird.

But, I can't help it. My brain doesn't work right.

I'm always trying new things. Wanting to accomplish something else. Getting up earlier every day to have more time and trying to get things done.

I have too many ideas and too little time. Maybe I have ADHD.

When I started treating addiction, people asked my why. "It's a choice, not a disease." "You can't help them." "They are beyond redemption." "They just need Jesus." "Aren't you just trading one addiction for another?"

When we became foster parents, people asked us why. "Don't you get attached?" "I could never do that." "I love kids too much to take them in and give them back." "Aren't you ruining your other kids' lives?" "How can you put your family at risk like that?"

I have a vision for the way I want my life to be. Not a picture. But a path. I follow the voice inside.

It's difficult to explain. It's like Taoism: "The tao that can be described isn't the real tao."

People are going to want to put you in a box and keep you there. That's just reality.

But, if you want to be free. If you want to have an impact. Then you will have to realize this important fact......

The path isn't always clear, it is cleared.

This philosophy has led me to interesting places, and I've met some interesting people. Like a homeless, Nicaraguan alcoholic with Miami gang ties. A 2 year old with dead beat parents, a vicious temper, and a non-curable medical condition. A 92 yr old matriarch with congestive heart failure and a fascination with my tattoos. A 16 yr old struggling with gender identity, bullying, and endocrine issues. An 8 yr old with a silver-toothed smile and a congenital heart defect.

Just stay on the path and see how things shake out.

"What's normal supposed to look like? No one's normal"

That's what a patient told me once, and I think she was dead on the money.

Folks that aren't in the world of drugs and addiction don't understand how much work it takes to get clean, stay clean, and live a somewhat normal life. (But there's that word again.)

So let's forget about normal.

Let's focus on something else.

Hope.

The most dangerous of all ideas.

This book is a 30 day devotional. It's not theology. It won't cure a disease or get you into heaven. I'm not a theologian, preacher, teacher, or any one else with qualifications to write such a thing.

It's about purpose over circumstances.

This book isn't for baptists, methodists, catholics, calvinists, dunkers, or sprinklers. It's for misfits, pill heads, lawyers, prostitutes, junkies, manic depressives, shut-ins, zealots, anarchists, tax-collectors, thieves, and insomniacs.

It's for those that are still searching.

And maybe that's you.

So sit back...

Relax...

And drink this book while reading your morning coffee

DAY 1

HELL

"Hell has a voracious appetite"
Proverbs 27:20
"Coyote is always out there waiting, and
coyote is always hungry"
--Navajo saying

Hell.

It's a hell of a way to start a book of devotions.

But I figure here is as good a place to start as any.

A lot of people reject religion because of hell. You know, eternal torment and such

Look, I get it. It's far from pleasant.

Which is why I'm starting the book this way.

Most of my life I thought about hell as God's little secret weapon for making us fall in line. Kind of like...."Yeah, you've got free will and all, but you better use that free will and do exactly what I say or else...."

Eternal torture and execution-style barbarism. These ideas where shaped by our medieval culture and somehow stayed around. But, what if Hell were something different? What if hell wasn't as much God's punishment but a prison of our own making?

Take a moment and consider the world around us. It is beautiful and cruel. A strange mix of birth and destruction. A cycle of death and renewal. And, if you look into people's lives, what will you find? A microcosm of this same circle. Heaven and Hell.

You see, hell can be a location you go or state of mind. Or maybe it's a presence you create for yourself and for others. This may be the only place that matters.

I've treated patients with depression that would swear every day was a living hell for them. If you saw their world, you'd think nothing of it. From the outside they would seem to have everything. Money, family, health. But, Hell was something inside them. Eating them from the inside out.

Hell's appetite is never quenched. It's always hungry. Always eating and devouring. Always looking for more.

For those that reject Christianity due to the concept of Hell, they must reject reality as well. Because Hell is as real as anything else.

You'll find it in a dark alley with a needle in it's arm. You'll find it in the case studies at the department of human services. You'll find it on the cancer ward at the children's hospital.

So today's mission is simple. Do nothing out of spite or envy or hatred or malice. Do not create hell on earth. Today's job is to live in a way that you make the world just a little better. Brighter. Fresher. Your job is to create Heaven, right here on earth. God's Kingdom.

Meditation

Spend 5 minutes meditating on Jesus's prayer.

"And he said unto them, When ye pray, say, Our Father which art in heaven, Hallowed be thy name. Thy kingdom come. Thy will be done, as in heaven, so in earth."
--Luke 11:2

DAY 2

RELIGION

"Pure religion that is undefiled before God and the Father is this: To visit the fatherless and widows in their affliction, and to keep himself unspotted from the world."
--James 1:27

I have a friend that doesn't like dogs.

And I mean, he really doesn't like them.

How can you not like dogs? That's what you're thinking, and it's a great question.

Dogs are loving, forgiving, protective, and decently self-sufficient. They give more than they take and ask for little more than the occasional belly rub and stick throw. They are what people should be.

Why is it so hard to meet the standard set by our canine friends?

To some extent, we all create our own religion. We do what we want and then justify the reasons later.

We start with the idea that religion is the way to some afterlife filled with riches. And our question is: How do we get there? But I believe this is the wrong question.

I believe the more important question is this: What's life all about?

And maybe our canine friends have answered this better than we ever could.

Here's the way of the dog:

It's vigilance to outside threats, a lick to local wounds, and sleeping at the foot of someone important.

It's serving a greater cause but not taking things too seriously. And of course... the occasional awkward sniff.

6

It doesn't get much better than a dog.

I read this about religion once, but I don't remember the source: Religion is our way of describing the shadows dancing on the walls.

This is an allusion to Plato's Cave.

You could say that it's our way to fill in the gaps to what we don't know.

I met Jesus once. He had the face of a homeless Nicaraguan man begging for change (and I refused to give him any). Maybe I will see him again some day. Or, maybe that was my only shot. My one chance to shake the hands of the divine.

Religion isn't our road to heaven. It's our road here on earth.

And here's my religion:

Black coffee, a home for orphans, rain on the roof, a kiss from my wife, the laughter of children, the desperation of the addict, the bond of blood and friendship, the mystery of science, the attraction of math, the calm of a forceful wind, the axe in your hand, and of course....the way of the dog.

I don't know much, but I know enough. I know that religion is more what you do than what you know.

Meditation

Spend 5 to 10 minutes in meditation by focusing on your breathing. As you inhale, smile and focus your intention:

Be happy, present in the moment, and full of life.

In other words....Be A Dog.

DAY 3

SO I LET IT GO...

I didn't always want to be a doctor.

What I really wanted was to be a rock star!

I wanted to play my guitar and sing my songs and travel the country in a beat up van.

But, I guess it wasn't in the cards. And my dreams for rock stardom changed to dreams of curing disease and helping the sick. I haven't looked back since.

I cut my hair. I gave up my rock n'roll dreams. I got married, had some kids, and got a real job.

And I'll tell you....it's been AMAZING! I have a great life and regret nothing.

But the truth is, I'm still a bit rebellious. I can't stand authority. I long for freedom and thirst for knowledge.

In my younger years, I debated all ideas about religion. Some debates were with people and some debates were just in my head.

Gnostic, agnostic, atheist, fundamentalist, calvinist, baptist, methodist, reformed, non-denominational, unitarian, buddhist. Labels are useless.

I've read, questioned, and puzzled my way through the Bible. I started in 7th grade by reading the Bible every day. This opened my eyes. I started to see that the "experts" often didn't know what they were talking about.

By high school, I had a large amount of knowledge about the stories in the Bible. In other words, I knew what the Bible said. But, this didn't mean that I knew what it meant.

My arrogance led me to have a faith that I couldn't quite live up to. Let me explain.

I was 20 years old and found out my nephew was dying. In fact, my sister-in-law was still pregnant, but the baby had a birth defect that would not allow him to live long outside of the womb.

So, I started to pray.

I knew that with faith he could be healed.

(I also knew that my brother was praying. And no one had more faith than my brother.)

When no miracle came, and my nephew died a few hours later, my faith died.

If prayers wouldn't be answered, then the Bible lied. Or Jesus lied. Or the whole thing was just one big scam.

So, I let it go. No more church. No more praying. No more god.

Looking back, I can see how that may seem silly or trivial. But, it was a huge turning point for me.

A couple years later and I'm living in Kansas City. I was in medical school and a newlywed. I met a friend that was a Christian, and we decided to check out a local church. I still had questions and doubts. But, for reasons I couldn't explain, I was being pulled back in.

The sleeper was awakened.

I learned that there was still a lot to learn. And maybe I didn't know everything after all.

I learned that death comes for us all.

I learned that faith is more than moving mountains, because some mountains are better climbed than moved.

I learned church isn't about a building or about rules. It's not a formula to some pie in the sky. It's about a path. A light in the darkness. A family. A community. A connection. A warm fire on a cold night.

My journey continues.

And I share this story with you to give you a brief glimpse behind the curtains.

I'm still a little rebellious. I like to challenge the status quo. I like to question WHY. I like to challenge people to think and to act.

And I've been kicked out of church twice.....well, almost.....

but that my friends is another story.

Meditation
Spend 5 to 10 minutes meditating. Start out by focusing on your breathing then consider what the following passage means:

"Awake, Oh Sleeper"
--Ephesians 5:14

DAY 4

Lawyers and their Damn Loopholes

Looking for a loophole he asked,
"And just how would you define 'neighbor'?"
--Luke 10:29

Leave it to a lawyer to look for a loophole.

What he really wanted... was an excuse. He wanted a reason to not do what needed to be done.

Jesus made it simple. So simple that people kill each other over the details. Love God. Help people out.

The educated man wanted to know who he was supposed to help. Sometimes it's best to not overthink things. You know what's right. You don't need a degree in religion to know who to help.

Earlier in the chapter, Jesus said the simple are the blessed ones, because they are the ones that "get it". God's grace.

This is the filter I use to see the world. A world that is full of difficulty and pain. But, also a world full of hope and beauty. Which world I live in is up to me. I can say "The kingdom of God is at the doorstep" or I can build a house of doubt, regret, and bitterness.

We can separate our tribes and throw rocks at each other, or we can make this world into something else.

I know it's more comforting to hold onto hate. To let anger shape your thoughts. To let your emotions run wild. To blame someone else for your misfortune. This is the easy road. The wide road.

But, there's a narrow way. A better way. And only a few find it.

The teachings of Jesus are simple but frustratingly difficult. Because he cuts to the heart of the matter every time. And, despite popular belief, there isn't a formula to follow. You can't just add his teachings to your life. You have to build your life from them.

He's either the cornerstone or he isn't.

You either build your house on the rock or you don't.

Quit worrying so much about your 10-year plan and worry about your today plan.

Or better yet...don't worry at all.

Hold onto God's abundance and vision.

Turn you worry into prayers of gratitude.

The road you walk is yours.

The adventure has already begun and, either way, you've got to put the miles in.

Let go of your expectations for other people and embrace this strange religion of serving your neighbor. Loving your enemy. And turning water into wine.

Keep it simple, stupid, and don't look for loopholes. Just walk the path. And see where it takes you.

<u>Meditation</u>

Spend 10 minutes meditating on the abundance of God. What this means is: God gives freely to all. There is enough. And what we give, we get back in multitudes. There are no loopholes. Keep it simple.

DAY 5

Your Mind Creates Your Reality

As I get older, I have become more and more fascinated with people's stories.

I am in a privileged position as people open up their lives to me. For example, it is quite common for patients to tell me, "you are the only person I can talk to".

What they mean is, other people don't listen. All they feel is judgement. What they mean is, they want to be accepted.

My wife once said that the best way to show someone that you care about them is to listen to their story....without condemning them.

(I'd probably also add...without giving advice, unless they ask.)

When you hear someone's story, you see their life from a completely different point of view than your own. You have a better understanding of their hurts, desires, and broken dreams. There is no place for judgement, only open ears.

Stories are important. Stories are powerful.

Stories are a good way to make a point.

Jesus knew this.

When pressed for his "life philosophy", Jesus summed it up like this: Love God, Love others. And to explain his philosophy deeper, he told stories. These stories were called parables.

Jesus's parables were both beautiful and strange. Their meanings often illusive. It's almost as if he left them open for interpretation.

You see, stories aren't just explanations of things. They become the things.

The stories we tell ourselves are our reality.

If you want to be happy but your story is sad, then you need to tell yourself a new story.

Your mind creates your reality.

Every day we wake up and decide what story we are going to live today. Where we'll focus our attention. What we'll consider valuable. What adventures we'll pursue.

What happens to you is not nearly as important as how you respond. Because bad things are going to happen, it's inevitable. But, what you do about those things will make you who you are. How you respond to the problems of life will be your story.

In a world of destruction, God asks us to be a part of creation.

In a world of chaos, God asks us to find discipline.

In a world living in the past, God asks us to embrace today.

In a world of lies, God asks us to speak truth.
In a world of orphans, God asks us to be a home.
In a world of pain, God asks us to sit with the dying.
In a world of suffering, God asks us to be a shelter.
In a world of darkness, God asks us to be a small light.
In a world of hate, God asks us to be Love.

Meditation

"God's kingdom is like a treasure hidden in a field for years and then accidentally found by a trespasser. The finder is ecstatic--what a find!--and proceeds to sell everything he owns to raise money and buy that field."

--Matthew 16: 44

Spend 10 to 20 minutes focused on your breathing.

DAY 6

MORE

"Wealth consists not in having great possessions, but in having few wants." --Epictetus

We want, we want, we want.

So many people are out there chasing happiness. A raise. A new job. A better car. A vacation. A lover. Retirement. Health. Kids. Success for their kids. More stuff, more things, more gadgets, more apps, the next phone, new pants, new bike, etc.

More stuff to make us happy. But, more leads us to feeling less. Less happy, less healthy, less good.

More junk in your life (physical or mental) only leads to stress, anxiety, helplessness, indecision, and apathy.

It seems there's always something else we need to be happy. Happiness is always around the corner. Just out of reach.

Rich people struggle with depression. Successful people suffer with anxiety. Spiritual leaders drown in addiction. We know this. But it seems we still think we would be the exception.

It's a bit of a paradox. If you can't be happy with what you have, you won't be happy with more. If you can be happy with what you have, you'll be happy with more, but it won't matter.

God gives us what we need. Take what you've been given. Be grateful. Be abundant. Spread love, and it will come back to you. Spread joy, and you will be happy.

The only things we need more of: **LOVE** and **TIME**.

Specifically, embracing the time we have. And, loving fully in this moment.

Give me that.

That's all I will ever need.

And, maybe a cup of coffee.

But, that's it.

Love, Time, and Coffee.

The End.

Meditation
What are you grateful for right now? Spend 10 to 20 minutes in prayer, focusing on gratitude. Be specific.

"I know what it is to be in need, and I know what it is to have plenty. I have learned the secret of being content in any and every situation, whether well-fed or hungry, whether living in plenty or in want. I can do all this through him who gives me strength."
--Philippians 4:12-13

DAY 7

Watch Yo' Mouth

"It's not what goes in the mouth. But what comes out."

Jesus said this.

He said that's what "defiles" us. He said that, out of the heart comes the things we say.

Now, some people try to distort this message. They want to make it something it's not. They want you to believe that he's telling people not to use foul language. Not to curse.

Well, that's bull$#!T.

There are no "bad words". Only better words. There is only bad intent.

Jesus was letting us know that the words you say betray how you feel inside. Your thoughts and beliefs influence the way you speak. And I believe the inverse is also true: The things you say influence the way you think and, in turn, influences the way you feel.

The words you use and the thoughts you have become your reality.

I am always worried when the first thing that comes out of someone's mouth is "I just want to be honest with you doc." It usually means they are not being honest or haven't been in the past. Who else has to warn you that they are being honest?

I am constantly lied to. It comes with the territory of treating addiction. When everyone seems to be trying to talk a good game, it can be a struggle to trust anyone.

I can't count how many times someone has told me, "I don't know why I ran out of meds." "I don't know how that showed up on my drug screen." "I'll never smoke meth again." "All those pills fell down the sink."

Just be honest, and you won't have to try and convince anyone.

Addiction fuels dishonesty. It's the nature of the beast. Lies destroy more homes than drugs do. And, if you agree with this, then you must see how powerful the words we say are.

If you want to get clean, clean this up first. Clean up your speech. Stop telling lies. Stop lying to yourself and stop lying to others.

You will never get better if you lie to yourself. And, if you lie to yourself enough, you will convince yourself that you are speaking the truth.

This is not a difficult principle to explain. Let me make it simple: No one likes a liar.

We all make mistakes. We have all bent the truth. But now, let's do something different.

We can make it our mission, starting today, to be the one that can be counted on. Relied on. Trusted. We will speak with integrity and honesty. We will use kind words. We will use our words to build up and not to tear down.

What we say and what we don't, speaks volumes about ourselves. And, it is an essential element of change and transformation.

Has someone ever lashed out at you? You knew it was because they were frustrated. You knew they didn't really mean the things they said. But it hurt anyway.

Words carry weight.

When under pressure, we often lose control of our mouth. Sometimes this takes the form of verbal abuse. Sometimes it takes the form of critical speech.

Do you know anybody that constantly complains? Always criticizing others. Constantly talking about their problems. It doesn't matter what you do for them, it's never enough. They could win the lottery but complain about the taxes they had to pay.

I try to teach my kids. I tell them to be the friend that they want to have. I tell them not to complain about circumstances but, instead, find something you can do to improve your situation. Don't talk bad about your friends behind their back. Be encouraging to others.

But am I taking this advice? Am I modeling this behavior for them? I must be the example, or else my words will fall flat.

Don't get caught up in gossip. Don't try to get "verbal" revenge on other people. It's not worth it. I have tried it. It rarely gets the results you want. If you are critical of others, then you are falsely comparing yourself to them. DON'T DO IT!

Some people are harsh and critical to the extreme. They say that they are just being "honest". Or just "telling it like it is". But, those are excuses they use. Let kindness be your guide in what you say.

There is a time for harsh speech and brutal honesty. You should stand for those that can't stand. Speak for those that can't speak. But patience, silence, and kind words go **A LONG WAY** in making the world a better place. Know your motivation and be intentional with your speech.

The verbal nonsense you utter about others can impair the way you see them. It's difficult to respect someone that you spent 15 minutes berating yesterday. It's difficult to be kind to someone that you don't respect. It becomes a vicious cycle. That person will be hurt. That person will not trust you. That person will be cold to you. And on and on it goes

Talk positive, Think positive.

Jesus said the things we say "defile" us. Defile means to desecrate or profane something sacred. He was teaching us to control our speech, but more importantly control our thoughts. Our minds are sacred. Treat them as such.

This goes for yourself as well. We all talk to ourselves. We all tell ourselves how to feel. And you can't verbally assault yourself without consequences.

How many times have you told yourself that you can't do something or that you just aren't as good as someone else? You tell yourself that you are a loser or that you will never succeed.

When you say it to yourself, you start to feel it in your entire body. You act as if it is true. You defile yourself.

Here are some examples of things people say

- I can't do this
- Things never go my way
- I can't catch a break
- I will never get better
- I don't have a problem with drugs
- My family understands, this is just who I am
- It's in my DNA to be an addict
- Nothing good will ever happen to me
- I have no education, I will never get a better job
- It's not my fault
- I am worthless
- It would be better for my family if I was dead

DON'T DO IT!

What you say to yourself is just as important as what you say to someone else. What you say MATTERS. If you say it enough, you will start to believe it.

You must believe in yourself. You must use your words and thoughts to build yourself up. To make yourself strong, courageous, bold.

Want to know how I do this?

I talk to myself.

Yeah, that's right......I said I talk to myself.

I'm not crazy. (At least I don't think I am.)

Control the inner dialogue in your brain by affirming a positive.

Don't focus on negative qualities (examples: I'm having a bad hair day, I'm always tired in the mornings, I think my co-worker hates me, I forgot to do such and such...I'm such an idiot.).

Focus on positive things. It doesn't matter if they are "true" or if you believe them. The more you repeat the mantras, the more they will come to be true. Your thoughts will jump out of your head and into reality.

Here's how you do it: Think about a characteristic that you want to be or something you are proud of. Write it down. Now meditate and picture it in your head. See yourself being that way.

Tell yourself what you are. I am unstoppable. I am successful. I am sober. I am kind to others. I have strong relationships. I am generous. I am grateful. (Repeat these phrases in your head multiple times. And repeat the process throughout the day.)

I personally don't write them down. But, I have heard from others that writing them down seems to help.

If you do this enough, your subconscious will start to believe it.

This is a form of prayer. You are praying for these things to come into your life.

I know this seems strange. But this ain't no hippie, new-age guru horse crap. This works! Trust me. We have the ability to change the world with our speech.

Your words and thoughts can actually help fix your problems. You just have to refuse to cave in to the heavy weight of negativity.

Positive thinking can actually make your life better. If you change the way you think about a situation, then your speech about it will change. And if you change your speech, you'll change the way you think about it.

Here's the deal....when you find yourself being overly negative about something, try to speak some type of positivity into it. This brings balance. It makes you feel better. And, it puts you back in control.

What's the right words?

- Speak up for justice
- Get rid of negative self-talk

- Use positive self-talk
- Say what you mean and mean what you say
- Use speech to rebuild relationships
- Always speak truth

Change your speech and you will change your attitude. Change your attitude and you change your life.

Think about how much you can improve your life just by controlling how you talk to yourself and to others. Think about being the person that stays positive (even in difficult times), the person that doesn't gossip, the person that's always honest. I think that kind of person has no choice but to have an awesome life.

Remember...

The world is full of a lot of bullshit.

You can make it better by the words you use.

Meditation
5 to 10 minutes focused on how you can use your words for good. Then 5 to 10 minutes focused on breathing.

DAY 8

What your track marks say about you...

Jesus answered them, "Many good works have I showed you from my Father; for which of those works do you stone me?" --John 10:32

Jesus.

They were out to get him.

For the things he said.

But, they were at a loss because of the things he did.

I had a patient tell me once that all that mattered to her was her daughter. Her track marks told another story.

Her life was a beautiful tragedy. And she kept playing it out over and over.

Her heart longed to bring goodness to her daughter. To be a light and a shelter in dark times. But in her own dark times, the pull was often too much. And she would surrender to the demons that penetrated her veins and flushed her brain with bitter-sweet chemicals.
....

Yesterday we talked about words. Today we talk about actions. Yesterday we talked the talk. Today we walk the walk.

I write this book, hoping my children will read it some day and better understand ME. But this book means nothing. It is only my life that I live daily that matters. Anything else is just window dressing.

Your life isn't what you say is true. It's what you do. Actions, reactions, attachments.

Faith isn't what you believe, but what you do. Faith is the life you live. It's why the Bible says that faith without works is dead.

If you want to change your life, change your actions.

The world is a cruel place. But most of the tragedy is man-made. Our selfishness is a disease. It spreads and infects the entire world.

Let me give you an example:

At the time of this writing, there are around 500,000 children in foster homes in the United States. Half a million kids that need good homes and guidance. If we choose to ignore this, not only do the children suffer, but they are more likely to grow up without hope, love, or any idea what a good family could look like. As adults, they are more likely to commit crime and end up in jail. And, the cycle continues.

At the time of this writing, approximately 840,000 people die every year due to lack of clean water and adequate sanitation. If you're like me, this statistic is shocking. Someone today will hold a small child that will die due to diarrhea from un-clean water. Could it have been avoided? What's our part?

"But wait a minute, Doc, not all suffering is man-made. What about natural disasters? Acts of God?"

You're right! Good point.

Recently there was a powerful hurricane that hit Florida. Massive destruction all around. And a good friend of mine is down there right now risking his life to get a small city's power back up and going. He's doing what he can to make a bad situation a little better for a small community.

Now, I know we can't save the world. We aren't the messiah. Jesus is. But God hasn't asked us to save anyone's soul. Only to be caretakers of his creation. This world was entrusted to us. Our hands to hold. If we ignore Jesus's commands to do good deeds and spread the good news, then we prove our lack of faith by our lack of action.

Like we said yesterday, the way you talk influences what you do. But life isn't about sitting around and talking. It's about doing. You don't have to do BIG things. Just do what you can. And let God work through you.

What does that look like? Well that will look different depending on your circumstances. Build your actions around love. Everything else will take care of itself.

A lot of people talk about Jesus. But he's just their get out of hell free card. They don't actually want to make any personal sacrifices, feed the hungry, touch the poor, or raise the dead. They want to sit

34

back in their reclining chair, watch Fox News, and criticize the rest of the world.

Now, don't think I'm judging anyone. I'm in the same boat. I feel the same inertia to apathy as well. But that's why I'm writing this. To remind myself...

Words matter. Thoughts matter. Actions matter.

Now, let's go do something that matters.

If your life isn't the way you want it to be. If you feel like you're stuck in a rut. If you feel lost. If you feel like you're searching for something you can't find. Just know this.....

If you want something different, do something different. Do something small that helps someone else and watch God's love work through your life and renew your spirit.

Your track marks tell a story.

But the ending of that story is up to you.

Make it a good one.

Meditation

Imagine all the people that God has put in your path. See them in your mind. Pray for God's blessing on them. Your children, your mother, your patients, your neighbors, orphans, widows, addicts, and deviants. Let your intent spread. Let your message be love.

DAY 9

ANXIETY

**"The first step: Don't be anxious. Nature controls it all. The second step: Concentrate on what you have to do. Fix your eyes on it. Remind yourself that your task is to be a good human being; remind yourself what nature demands of people. Then do it, without hesitation, and speak the truth as you see it."
--Marcus Aurelius**

Sounds good, Marcus. But what do you know?

Oh yeah...that's right, you were ruler of the world.

Ol' Marcus might have been onto something.

We live and we die. All of us slaves to the universe. The raging storms and chaos of life hit whether we are prepared or not.

So, the only thing we can really do is the job right in front of us.

This is the control we have. We can be good to others, and we can be true to ourselves.

Anxiety over an unforeseen future serves no purpose. Mourning a distant past is just as useless. These things keep us captive to an imagined existence and hold hostage our peace of mind. We must overcome the past and the future. We must live in the NOW. The real world. With all our real problems. And face them with courage.

This doesn't mean: don't plan for the future. It doesn't mean: Don't learn from the past. It just means: Don't worry so damn much about it.

Jeremiah 29:11 says, "For I know the plans I have for you". This line has been copied and pasted everywhere. From T shirts to coffee cups. But, sometimes I forget it's meaning.

Here's how Peter said it "be content with who you are, and don't put on airs. God's strong hand is on you....Live carefree before God; he is most careful with you."

I think he is saying: I may be nothing more than a speck of dust, but I can still do what is right in the moment. I don't have to be "important". I just have to be. Because, that's enough for God. God's love is infinite and perfect. And that's enough for me. In a world full of madness, I can keep calm and trust in God's purpose for me.

It ain't always easy. But it's always worth it.

I only have control of myself. My actions. My thoughts. This moment in time. Not nature. Not chaos. Not death. Not cancer. Not destruction.

And maybe.... that's enough.

Meditation

"For this reason I say to you, do not be worried about your life, as to what you will eat or what you will drink; nor for your body, as to

> what you will put on. Is not life more than food, and the body more than clothing?"
> --Matthew 6:25

Spend 10 minutes. Just breathing. Focus on your breath. Push other thoughts aside. Let go of your anxiety and worry. At least for these 10 minutes. You can pick them back up when you're done. Let the

present moment be enough.

DAY 10

Ideas are Dangerous

"And she brought forth her firstborn son, and wrapped him in swaddling clothes, and laid him in a manger"
--Luke 2:7

Ideas are dangerous.

Our lives are the paths we walk as we try to decide which ideas are worth following.

Christmas isn't a holiday. It's an idea.

Which is why it has shaped our minds over the years. It's why writers, poets, and artists have focused so much time and attention to capture the idea of Christmas.

I like to say Merry Xmas. Mainly.....because I like to see people get triggered.

"Don't take the Christ out of Christmas!", they say.

X is the greek letter chi. The first letter in the name Christos. And it's been used to represent Christ for a long time.

It's interesting how Christmas has changed over the years.

In the Middle Ages, it was like Mardi Gras. A big party.

Considered pagan by the Puritans, there was a time that it was outlawed in England (and Boston). But you can't keep a good holiday down, and soon it was back. It became a national holiday for us on June 26, 1870. Trees, stocking, caroling, manger scenes, lights. And now, ugly sweaters, cheap gifts, and watered-down egg nog.

The history of its pagan roots is interesting. A celebration of the end of winter and hard times, and the return of the sun. (If you look closely, you might find a metaphor there.)

For many people, Christmas is about time with family. But the truth is, for some, there is no family to gather with. There are no good memories to cherish. It is only another day on the calendar.

Normally when I write, I have an audience in mind. Someone I'm thinking about. Maybe it's a patient that's struggling with addiction, or a stranger fighting depression, or an old friend dealing with his doubts and failures. But this time, I'm just writing.

There are a lot of people that don't believe. They don't believe in God, they don't believe in Christmas, they don't believe in themselves. But even in this dark night, there's a small light burning.

Maybe it's a wish. Maybe it's a dream. Maybe it's something deeper.

I don't know where I'm going with this, except that I had something I wanted to say about Christmas.

And this is what I wanted to say:

Humans have a tendency to muck things up.

We have history of creating hell on earth. For ourselves and for others.

Christmas is our celebration of the opposite. Heaven coming to earth.

No matter where you are this Christmas, I want you to know this message.

In the strangest of places.

A promise.

Hope.

A way to redemption.

A baby.....sleeping in a manger.

Meditation

Mediate on the idea of heaven coming to earth. Even if you're going through dark times: depression, addiction, cancer. Light can shine through.

DAY 11

Tax Collectors (and others of ill repute)

There are a few things you never want to be in life.

1. Thief
2. Murderer
3. IRS agent

We could probably add more to this list, but I want to keep it short. I prefer focusing on what you should do, instead of what you shouldn't.

Maybe I'm being too harsh on tax collectors.

And maybe today's tax collectors aren't as bad as they used to be. But I'm going to keep them on the list. They've never had a good reputation. Just read the Bible and see for yourself.

Back in Jesus's day, they weren't actually paid a salary (as far as I know). But they were given the task of getting the money. And whatever extra they could extract, that was theirs. If you couldn't pay, they could lend you a little (with a hefty interest tacked on). Almost like a state-sanctioned bookie. Except they never paid out, just took in.

In the Bible, they worked for the enemy empire.

To help keep the people down.

To keep the people broke and powerless.

They were traitors to their country, their religion, and their family. They were hated.

But, in walks Jesus.

And he takes a seat at the table.

It's not the healthy that need a doctor, but the sick.

So he takes these traitors and offers them a new chance. To change their lives forever. And some take him up on it.

And in the mix of helping the sick and destitute, Jesus tells us life is a feast.

A party.

A thing to celebrate.

While we can.

While we have the opportunity.

There will be plenty of time to mourn.

To fast.
To be silent.
But now...
Now is the time for celebration.
For eating and drinking.
For singing and dancing.
For living with purpose.
For answering the call.
For healing the sick.
For kingdom come.

Meditation

And He also told this parable to some people who trusted in themselves that they were righteous, and viewed others with contempt "Two men went up into the temple to pray, one a Pharisee and the other a tax collector. The Pharisee stood and was praying this to himself: 'God, I thank You that I am not like other people: swindlers, unjust, adulterers, or even like this tax collector. I fast twice a week; I pay tithes of all that I get.' But the tax collector, standing some distance away, was even unwilling to lift up his eyes to heaven, but was beating his breast, saying, 'God, be merciful to me, the sinner!' I tell you, this man went to his house justified rather than the other; for everyone who exalts himself will be humbled, but he who humbles himself will be exalted."

--Luke 18:9-14

Spend 10 to 20 minutes meditating. Picture your body surrounded by a warm light. Imagine everything as it needs to be. The warm light is love. The light is truth. It connects to you and spreads.

DAY 12

Travel Hacking Tips from Nicaragua

I'm 30,000 feet in the air.

Looking out the airplane window.

Somewhere over Central America.

The mountains of Nicaragua are getting closer.

Sometimes we find ourselves in places we didn't expect and have no better explanation than the most obvious. But let me back up for a second. I need to tell you a few more details of how we took...
 the longest trip ever.

Our plane was to fly from Tupelo to Nashville to Houston to Managua.

We get to Nashville. We get ready to leave for Houston. There's a delay. No big deal.

Eventually, we get on the plane. We wait. We wait some more. Then the pilot tells us that the Houston airport has closed temporarily due to weather. So, we get off the plane. No more flights to Houston tonight. We have to stay in Nashville. Fly out tomorrow.

But our flight from Houston to Nicaragua is gone.

As Woody Allen brilliantly put it, "If you want to make God laugh, tell him about your plans."

Our team has to split up. 3 will fly to Costa Rica to then hit the connector to Nicaragua. The other 5 fly to Miami to hit the connector to Nicaragua. No problem.

But in Miami, we hit another snag. We were never actually assigned seats on the Nicaragua plane. United blames Copa. Copa blames United. We are stuck in the middle. Or... in Miami to be more exact. And there's no escaping it, we're staying the night in Miami. They give us a flight the next day to Managua. We go to print our boarding passes. They won't print. After debating with the Copa representative, he finally agrees to check the computer. We aren't assigned seats. He says it's a problem with United.

We go back to United. They tell us Copa overbooked and won't fess up. Round and round we go.

Now, staying in Miami doesn't sound so bad, but it takes 5 hours to get this whole mess straightened out, and it's late. We make the most of it, Uber to a restaurant, and then get back to the hotel.

Need to be up the next morning by 4am. No South Beach for us.

United Airlines helps us out. They get us a room at the hotel airport. They give us $90 food vouchers. They clean up the mess Copa Airlines made. They get us a flight to Panama.

From Miami we fly to Panama. From Panama we fly to Nicaragua. We make it to Managua and then drive the 4hrs to La Dalia. We are 2 days behind.

But what are you going to do? You can't control the weather. Or airlines. Or other humans. Only your attitude and actions. You can only do what you can do.

When asked why he went to Nicaragua, a missionary once replied, "Because you won't". The point is not that everyone should. And I don't want to put words in his mouth, but I think what he was saying was, you've got to do something. And for him, it was Nicaragua.

I want to tell you the story of a boy named James. And the first thing I should tell you is that his name is not James. But that's not what's important.

James doesn't know how old he is. He doesn't know when his birthday is. He doesn't know where his parents are. He doesn't have a clue what the future holds.

He says he's 15 years old. I'd say 12 or 13 at the oldest.

He's been an orphan for years. Living on the streets of Nicaragua. Begging for money and food.

He was taken in by a group and dropped at a drug and alcohol rehab facility. A facility that is more like a self-sufficient village. It's a non-government organization and survives on donations and small payments from those that can. They raise livestock and grow their own crops. They attempted to grow coffee, but the first crop wasn't successful and now it will take another 3 years.

The rehab is underfunded and understaffed.

Sometimes government agencies bring orphans to stay. It's safer than the streets. Food, water, clothing.

James is dropped off with the thought he will be picked back up at some time and taken to a family to care for him. But this doesn't happen.

James is at the rehab a few months, when the unthinkable happens. He is raped by 3 men.

The rehab is voluntary for some. But there are also those that the courts have sent there. So in the mix you have people seeking recovery, convicts, addicts, and orphans.

But what choice is there? What choice is left for James? There's no home to go to.   There's no family waiting.

Nicaragua is a lot like America, there's just not a lot of people willing to take in orphans.

Another doctor once asked me why go to a third world country to practice medicine for a week. It can not possibly do any long term good. One week of care makes little difference in the grand scheme of things.

Here's what I used to think: Everything changes if I go this week, he goes the next, then someone else the next, etc. Because the lack of justice in the world is nothing more than willing inaction. So I can't wait for him to take action. Because I can only control my actions, not his.

But maybe it has nothing to do with that. Maybe it's all about James. The boy with the lost past, the tortured present, and the unknown future.

Maybe just hearing his story, being there to listen, to care, to heal: Maybe that is the beginning. The beginning to something else.

A future not yet dreamed of.

We can close our eyes or keep them wide. The choice is ours. To make the world what it will be.

Meditation

"Give your entire attention to what God is doing right now and don't get worked up about what may or may not happen tomorrow."
--Matthew 6:34

DAY 13

No Staff, No Bag, No Bread, No Money.....No problem

We have been sold a lie.

We bought it hook, line, and sinker. There is no one to blame but ourselves.

What were we sold? What did we buy? An idea.

The idea that we are incomplete. And because of this, we long for more. We constantly seek out more. More is all we know. And more is never enough.

More keeps us hungry, but never full. More keeps us up at night. It keeps us broke and ashamed. It artificially elevates our confidence before dropping us low. We drown in the more and long for more. We are our own enemies.

But there is a way out. A way so simple and obvious. The way is this: Less.

We live in a world of chaos. Turmoil and confusion.

You do not have to complicate your life in order to save it. You do not have to turn to drugs or alcohol to escape. You must only live. It's simple.

By reading this, you are already preparing yourself to be a warrior. You are ready for battle. You understand it starts with your inner voice, your mind, and your spirit. Your body and soul.

But knowledge is just the beginning. Now, we take action. We clean up our lives.

Our past comes with a lot of baggage. I dream for a day when kids grow up in homes that they don't feel the need to escape from. When childhood memories are pleasant. When the past brings a smile. But for many people, reality is a darkness all too real.

If your inner life is cluttered with bad memories and regret, then this spills over to your physical surroundings.

It's time to clean it up. It's time to simplify.

Get rid of clutter and excess. Embrace the minimal amount needed to make you happy. Clean up your house, internal and external.

What does this mean?

I have 4 children (sometimes 5). We have a lot of stuff. I am horrible at simplifying my life. With 7 people living together, it can be difficult. I am the the world's worst minimalist.

So, this is how our family attempts to do our best: We live beneath our means, we give to the poor, and we save. We look to experiences over material possessions. We aren't perfect, and it's not a competition. I don't tell you this to brag, but to show you that our lives may look different, but we can have the same mission. To live a simple life.

I wish I could say our house was spotless, surfaces empty and clean. But the truth is, it feels impossible at times to avoid the

accumulation of clutter. Normally our floors are covered in toys.
Someone once said it looked like Christmas threw up in our house.
(I'm still not sure if she meant this as a complement, an insult, or just
a statement of fact. What's funny is I don't think it was that messy.
She just had no experience with a lot of kids running wild and
playing with their toys in the living room.)

I had a friend tell me once that he was a minimalist too. He was
poor, he said... and then laughed.

The truth is, simplifying your life doesn't mean going without. It
means HAVING. It means HAVING the right things.

But what are these things?

The things that matter.

We ignore our health, our dreams, and our relationships.... while we slave away to buy things that rot, break, and are eventually thrown away.

Living simply can mean different things for different people. I know
what it means for me.

Start with the excess. All the "stuff" you have. Keep what you need
and love and get rid of the rest. This act of reduction is a metaphor
in a sense. Something you do in the real world that has deeper
implications.

It's the cleaning up of your soul.

You are shedding your attachment to material possessions. And by doing this, you will start to understand what makes you happy and what doesn't. What things in life actually bring joy and which ones are an illusion.

When you see behind the curtain, you realize how fragile our existence is. You've spent years wasting away. It is time to waste no more.

In Luke 9:3, Jesus said to his disciples, "Take nothing for your journey, no staff, nor bag, nor bread, nor money". And in a similar way, I want you to take as little as possible.

This material world no longer chains you to it.

Have all you need in life. Have all that brings you joy. No less. No more.

There are too many choices in life. So many choices, that we have decision fatigue. Paralysis by analysis.

Much of your life can be simplified by just taking away choices. This is not to limit you, but to free you. To free you from the mindless drudge of existence and welcome you to your life. The life you carve out from this point on. A simple life, free from drugs, anxiety, depression, regret.

Start with a blank slate. Create any picture you want. Your life, your goals, your values, your vision.

Your life is like a cup. It will only hold so much before it starts to spill over. You decide what to put in your cup.

You decide what gets to spill over.
Meditation
God fill us with what we need. No more. No less. Amen.

DAY 14

A psalm of no consequence

A psalm of no consequence

I am grateful.

I am grateful for the abundance in my life.

I am grateful that I have been delivered from my enemies. No harm has come to me. I know that any slights have been counted and processed and will work for my good.

I know that you are with me. And that dark times will be brought to light.

Happiness is mine.

Love is mine.

Riches are mine.

You have delivered them into my hands. To enjoy and to share.

My enemies came to snatch them away, but you are the wise one. You are the strong one. No one comes to the master's house without a welcome. And the party has begun.

My eyes can see.

My cup is full.

And my heart has gladness to give.

I see my family. I see my sons. I see my daughters. I see my son's sons. I see my daughter's daughters.

My family will grow. My descendants will cover the earth. They will find happiness where they go and carry your light with them.

I am grateful for what I see of my future. I am content to live in the present. Your goodness is with me always.

Selah.

DAY 15

HOW TO SURVIVE ANYTHING

The truth is: we all suffer. Just in different ways.

"Healthy" people die suddenly. Traumatic brain injuries turn adults into children. Back pain. Diabetes. Children with tumors. Heart attacks. The decay of dementia. And everything in between.

Everyone's story is unique. But at the same time, similar. Because we're all in this together. Living and dying.

And, on a long enough timeline, all results are the same. No one gets out alive.

But mixed in to these moments of pain and despair is a life full of beauty, promise, magic, and redemption.

I have a patient that has been battling metastatic breast cancer for 2 decades.

That's 20 years she's spent with death whispering it's bitter lullaby into her ear.

Before she was ever born...the cards were stacked against her. Her mother never wanted a baby. She had surgery to prevent pregnancy (it obviously didn't work). She tried to get an abortion (but was too far along). So a little girl was born into a world that didn't want her. And she grew up strong and didn't even know it. She was a fighter.

10 years ago she was told her cancer was not curable. And thus began a journey of experimental chemo and hope. And so far....she's a walking miracle.

20 years since her diagnosis and 10 years since being given a death sentence....she speaks to groups as a survivor. Her fight, her struggle, her life.....has become an inspiration to others.

So what's the point of survival anyway? When our path leads to destruction no matter what we do?

Because life is meaningful. YOUR LIFE is meaningful!

I am not saying all things happen for a reason. I am saying that life and death happens, no matter what you do.

Life sucks and then you die. This is reality. But there's something else to it. Something in the cracks of existence that calls to us.

You can't control the things that happen to you. But you can control how you respond. And what you believe.

Don't worry about being strong.

Instead: Be brave. Be persistent. Be fierce.

You're reading this and that means you're alive. And if you're alive, you still have time.

Think about the impossibility of existence. The earth is at just the right distance from the sun. Your ancestors survived earthquakes, tornadoes, famine, ice storms, wooly mammoths, the plague, the flu, depression, addiction, poison, drought. They survived against all odds to reproduce. Your parents had to choose each other over every other mate in the world. Your genetic code had to line up just right. You had to survive in the womb.

If you don't believe you have a purpose, then you aren't paying close enough attention.

What's more arrogant to say? We have a purpose? Or....We're an accident?

When you understand all the forces and factors that had to be perfect just to bring you here..... then maybe you will start to see: You are a walking miracle as well.

BY DEFINITION: YOU ARE A SURVIVOR.

The things that brought you here may have been painful. But this is where you are. It doesn't mean this is who you are. Just where you are. You get to pick who.

Life isn't always easy. It sure isn't fair. But it's an adventure worth taking.

My patient shouldn't be here.

All the cards have been stacked against her.

But she's not done yet.

Because she's a survivor.

How about you?

Meditation
"Peace to you. Just as the Father sent me, I send you."
John 20:21
Spend 10 to 20 minutes focused on God's peace.

DAY 16

Heavy Metal Music and Hardcore Religion

"What do you people mean by going around the country repeating the saying, 'The parents ate sour grapes, and the children's teeth are set on edge?' As sure as I'm the living God, you're not going to repeat this saying in Israel any longer. Every soul-man, woman, child--belongs to me, parent and child alike. You die for your own sin, not another's."
--Ezekiel 18:1-4

I'm writing this while listening to heavy metal.

My oldest, she doesn't like rock music.

I admit it....I've failed as a parent.

I know this, yet I carry on.

What other choice do I have?

I have 4 kids, sometimes 5. Raised the same, but none of them are alike. Everyone is different. And that is a beautiful fact.

The sour grapes parable (mentioned in the scripture above) was this idea that you suffered for the sins of your ancestors. I'm not 100% sure where the idea came from, but I can imagine. The religion started with Adam eating some bad fruit. The next thing you know, all the descendants are cursed. "Teeth set on edge."

This isn't far-fetched. I'm an addiction doctor and a foster parent. I see the mistakes of the parents and I see how the children suffer. So in a sense it's true. You eat some bad fruit, and your kids get the stomach ache as well. But what's interesting is the scripture gives us another option.

I'm not a Calvinist, and I don't believe in total depravity or original sin. Because you don't die for Adam's sin. You die for yours.

Too many people think sin as something that has consequences after you die. But the consequences are here and now as well.

Self destruction isn't just a steep slope. It's also the gradual decline. It's telling that small lie, over, and over, and over again. It's the slow transformation into a person unrecognizable as the one you want to be. It's not fulfilling your potential. It's leaving God's path for your own.

And sometimes we find ourselves in places we never imagined we'd end up. Like my patient that was raped at 15 and started taking her mom's pain pills. Which led to meth amphetamines and heroin. Which led to prostitution. Which led to getting pregnant. And now she has a choice. Get clean or sacrifice her child to the god of destruction.

Teeth set on edge. Kids paying for the parents mistakes.

But what's important about this scripture is not the sin. It's the redemption. It's God saying that, sure as he's a living God... He's God of the living. And the living have a choice.

Depending on what you're going through, salvation can feel like a fairy tale. I think this is something a lot of religious leaders forget. Real religion meets real people with real problems and offers a real solution.

Listen, I know you've had serious problems.

I know your parents treated you like shit.

I know you lost your way somewhere down the road.

But you aren't your parents.

You aren't their bad choices.

You aren't their cruel intent or their reckless neglect.

You aren't their drugs.

You aren't their slurs.

You aren't their fists.

You are you.

You've survived unimaginable pain.

And now, destined for great things.

The sour grapes will no longer turn your stomach.

As surely as God lives....you are free to choose exactly who you want to be.

My kid may not like heavy metal, but that's okay. Because I don't want her to be me.

I want her to be something else.

Something greater than I ever could have imagined.

Something only God truly knows.

What about you?

What are you becoming?

Meditation
I pray for God's grace over my children. Let the path unfold. Let our choices be ours. And let us choose life.

Spend 10 to 20 minutes praying for either your children or the abandoned children of the world. Ask God if he is leading you to become a foster parent.

DAY 17

Out of the Abyss

"You are going to die there", the voice said to me.

I was getting ready to go to work, but in a week I was leaving for Haiti on a medical mission trip.

The voice wasn't audible. It was inside my mind. Was this my subconscious running wild? Was it my fear expressing itself? Was it a warning? Was it an evil presence trying to persuade me not to go? I didn't know.

So, I did what anyone would do, I packed my bags and left. I didn't go in spite of the voice. I didn't go because of the voice. I didn't assume the voice was crazy. I went, fully expecting it to be true.

I went because that is where I felt I should be.

Dying in pursuit of purpose is better than living forever in the abyss of complacency.

This isn't some type of humble brag about bravery or courage. I never felt unsafe in Haiti. I never even came close to anything dangerous. So, the initial thoughts about dying were completely ludicrous.

In Haiti, people crowded around the clinic. There was no way to see everyone that needed to be seen. I remember a lady holding her baby through the window, hoping someone would take it and help.

We had to take one man to the local hospital. They wanted a bribe to let him use the oxygen tank that they had.

I have heard it said that resourcefulness is more important than resources.

Sometimes the only "health care" you can give is to care. Taking the time to sit and listen. It matters here, and it matters there. People are the same. People need connection. People want to know you care.

I would ride in the back of the truck to the clinic. One of our translators would point out things on our way. He told me Haiti was a great place to live if you had any money. I looked around and didn't see anyone that would fit that description.

The streets were crowded at times. We would give kids rides to school. We would watch the animals in the streets. We would see the filth that they made and how all the people had to walk through it to get to work.

But don't let this brief description give you the wrong idea. It was also a very beautiful place with beautiful people. It's interesting how you can see something from different angles. It had a magic about it. A mystery.

We met a guy that was traveling the world. He was currently exploring Haiti. He was from England. He told us, "I guess I picked a bad time". He was talking about the earthquake. I found him fascinating. He was not scared of discomfort or uncertainty. He was living his life. He didn't let little things like earthquakes, political unrest, or violence stop him from following his path.

We met some missionaries. They were helping at an orphanage.

We met local spiritual leaders. They would help decide who was the sickest in the community and who needed our help the most.

Not all the spiritual leaders were supportive though. One night, on a small mountain outside of our compound, we saw smoke rising. It burned the next day as well. We were later told that it was a local voodoo priest burning a sacrifice to put a curse on us.

I don't know if this was true or not. They may have just been trying to pull one over on us. But it makes for a good story.

I ate goat for the first time in Haiti.

I ate strange looking bone-in fish.

Our compound had a picture of Wyclef Jean at the bar. He had stayed at this hotel before.

We saw a lot of patients at the various make-shift clinics. Our team leader would try to keep up with the numbers. Everyone had a card. I would often "work in" family members of the patients I was seeing. I would write down their info on the back of the card. This made it difficult for the team leader to keep track. I didn't care. How could I say no to these people?

One clinic was in an unfinished hotel. There was no ceiling or walls. Just cinder blocks and foundation. There was an unfinished pool. It made me wish I had brought a skateboard.

I learned how to ask several basic medical questions in Creole. And, sometimes, I was able to understand the answer.

We saw the capital building that had been ravaged by the quake. We saw tent cities. We saw crime. We saw poverty and kindness and humanity.

We saw the mix of the world, right there in one of the world's poorest countries.

But this devotion isn't about Haiti at all. It's about how you respond. How you respond to the voice inside your head. How do you follow your purpose? Will you follow it to the ends of the earth? Will you chase it down and conquer it? No matter what fears you have, will you see them through?

Because I can tell you that it's worth it.

And when the voice calls out "you are going to die there", will you answer...

"So be it."

Meditation

"God's love is meteoric,
   his loyalty astronomic,
His purpose titanic,
   his verdicts oceanic.
Yet in his largeness
   nothing gets lost;
Not a man, not a mouse,
   slips through the cracks."

--Psalm 36:5-6

DAY 18

THE 3 MINDS

He was 14 when he started using.

I looked him in the eye and asked what happened.

He told me about his mother.

He told me about the abuse.

He told me about the burn marks, the lack of food, the lack of sleep, the long nights waiting.

He wasn't saying it like it was an excuse. Just an answer to a question.

And here the road splits. What path to go down?

He chose escape. No judgement here. But now, we must confront the demons if we want to be free. Confront and destroy. It's the only way.

Jesus once taught that you have to see what is in front of you before you can see anything else.

To know yourself. Self Truth.

Buddha said it like this: "Be a lamp unto yourself."

It's our subconscious that seeks to protect us. Our conscious pretends to be in control. Our conscience lights the path. And those are the 3 minds that spin a web inside our brain and our soul.

The 3 Minds
1) Conscious
2) Subconscious
3) Conscience

Repair the 3 minds. Learn to control them. And instead of being a slave to re-action, be a person of pro-action.

Bring your mind out into the open.

Know who you are. Follow the path. And become who God set you apart to be.

The path may not be clear. It may have to be cleared.

Do not let your beliefs be the truth. Let the truth be your beliefs.

It is the only way.

Meditation

"But all things become visible when exposed by the light, for
everything that comes visible is light."
--Ephesians 5:13

Spend 10-20 minutes focused on your breathing. Picture your breath
as white light flowing inside and circulating around. Believe that
you can be healed. And see it in your mind. Allow the white light to
flow.

DAY 19

LIFE after DEATH

Lately I've been thinking a lot about death.

I don't mean to be morbid. But recently I was slapped in the face with the cold hard fact that we live here in finite terms. You can play by all the right rules. It doesn't matter. It's coming for you and for me.

The sneak attack, the blitzkrieg, the slow spiral. It comes in many forms. I've seen them all. It's somewhat hard to escape.

I've held hands with those dying. I've comforted the family of those passed. And most recently, I lost a close friend.

I don't care so much about me. But I do care when it happens to those I love. This isn't altruistic. It's quite selfish. I like the people in my life to hang around.

You have probably been told to live as if today is your last day. But I think we should live as if today is everyone else's last day. How would that change us? What would our interactions be like? What words would we use with other people? our children? our spouse? our friends?

Death brings a strange gift to those still living.

What would happen if we stopped worrying about things out of our control?

What if we had the courage to do things that we wanted to do, not afraid of what other people think?

What if we let anxiety about the future just slip away, and we lived content in the present moment? Accepting fate as it came.

We can't go back and change the past. We can't add more time. We can't change the way we were. But, we can change the NOW. We can be present. We can love more fully. We can focus on the things in our control and not dwell on those outside of it.

And maybe that's what I've been doing lately. Maybe I've been thinking too much about death and not enough about life.

Because I can't change death, but I can change life.

I can be there for others. I can listen. I can help.

I can do more for myself as well. I can read more, write more, learn more. I can grow. I can laugh. I can surround myself with people that make me happy. I can say no to things that weigh me down and yes to things that bring joy.

I refuse to waste this precious time, for I don't know how much of it is left.

I was at a funeral recently. A celebration mass at a catholic church. At one point we were all standing up and holding hands. I was staring at the picture of one of my best friends and holding the hand of another. I couldn't help but think: This is the life after death. We are living it now. I am not saying it in some type of religious way. I am not talking about heaven. I am just talking about now. Today.

What we have left of ourselves, our family, our friends, and our little time.

This is the gift that death brings. It opens our eyes to life.

Meditation
"If we humans die, will we live again? That's my question.
  All through these difficult days I keep hoping,
  waiting for the final change--for resurrection!
Homesick with longing for the creature you made,
  you'll call--and I'll answer!
You'll watch over every step I take,
  but you won't keep track of my missteps.
My sins will be stuffed in a sack
  and thrown into the sea--sunk in deep ocean."
--Job 14: 14-17
Spend 10-20 minutes meditating on the gift of life.

DAY 20

How to Conquer Crippling Anxiety

He tells me that in prison, you either pick a side or you die.

He shows me his tattoo. Some type of racist symbol. The ink fading into a dullish green hue. The color of apathy. The color of discontent. A reminder of his hate. Hate born from a need to survive.

I have this belief that you don't have to understand or agree with someone to listen.

He clings to his misguided crutch and limps along.

He tells me he had almost completely changed his mind. But his trust was broken, and he allowed the hate to take back control.

Easier to blame someone else than to look inside.

Fear blinds us to love.

Fear deafens us to compassion.

Fear paralyzes us to right action.

There's a story in the Bible about a rich man that had, for all intents and purposes, lived a good life. But there was one thing that he lacked. One thing that he could not escape.

He was rich and too afraid to leave his money behind.

It's a story about having everything but still having nothing.

It's a story about faith. But it's also a story about fear.

There's a saying in the Buddhist world (I'm unsure of the origins) that there are 3 requirements for Zen: Great Faith, Great Doubt, and Great Perseverance.

I like that.

The opposite of faith is not doubt. The opposite of faith is fear.

In our world of science, religious faith has been replaced. There is not much that we can't explain with theories and experiments. Our world is concrete.

And, if our faith in this god of science is so great, then why do we continue to have so much fear?

You don't have to answer that. (It was rhetorical.)

Now, I want to take you down a slightly different direction. Because all this talk about faith was to set up our conversation about fear. And the talk about fear was to connect us to our anxiety.

So, for some reading this, it will be about faith.

For others, it will be about fear.

But for most, it will be about anxiety. The kind that keeps you inside. The kind that keeps you from living the life you want. The kind that smothers your relationships and buries your dreams.

How to Conquer Fear and Crippling Anxiety

1) Live Carefree

"So be content with who you are, and don't put on airs. God's strong hand is on you; he'll promote you at the right time. Live carefree before God; he is most careful with you."

--1 Peter 5:6-7

It will do you no good to pretend your anxiety does not exist, or that it's useless to you. Your anxiety is there for a reason. And it's okay.

Be content with who you are and where God has you. You might not be perfect, but God's plan for you is.

Fear is a survival mechanism. You are alive, which means it worked. Thank it for a job well done.

I want you to understand a connection.

Your body. Becomes. Your mind.

Your mind. Becomes. Your body.

They are one and the same.

There are patterns of connection all through life. Everyone we meet. Everyone we see. Every road we travel. Every thought we think. All connected. All energy. Dissipating and accumulating.

The twisting spirals of our lives are not accident or chance.

They are meaning.

Meaning is a noun and a verb. It is to be lived with brutal abandon to the frivolous nature of material existence. It is a reproach to the mundane.

In this present moment is the place you find yourself. You are not your past. You are not your future. You are here.

To overcome anxiety, learn to be here now. Practice mindfulness and conscious action. This means when you do something, do it with purpose or don't do it at all.

God's strong hand is on you. Live carefree before God, because he is most careful with you. (I couldn't have said it better myself.)

2) A seed can grow.

When people asked Jesus about faith, he would tell them all they needed was a mustard seed.

A seed is a cocoon. A seed can become something else entirely.

It can become a plant that birds find shelter in.

In other words, even in our fears of inadequacy, we can become something that helps others find shelter and hope.

And that my friends is what it's all about.

We are the connections.

The shelter. The storm.

The chaos. The calm.

The roots and the vine.

The grape and the wine.

God asks us to be his hands and feet. To work the garden of hope and know that in time...the harvest comes.

3) Be still

I just finished my morning meditation. Now I'm drinking coffee and watching a purple sunrise.

Over the past 2 years, I've been getting deeper into meditation.

Meditation connects you to the moment like nothing else can.

Meditation is a form of prayer.

Your mind is uncontrollable. Your thoughts are wild and untamed.

By sitting. By being still. By making your mind surrender to your will, you will find a sense of connection and control that most people will never know.

"Don't fret or worry. Instead of worrying, pray. Let petitions and praises shape your worries into prayers, letting God know your concerns. Before you know it, a sense of God's wholeness, everything coming together for good, will come and settle you down. It's wonderful what happens when Christ displaces worry at the center of your life."

--Philippians 4:6-7

I like these verses because it points out something interesting, you take your worries and shape them into something else. Something useful.

Asking God for help is one thing. But, the scripture is also clear that we should include praises. Most people think this means "praising God". Maybe singing, music, worship, etc. But I think it means gratitude.

Finding contentment with where you are. Being thankful for what you have instead of concerns about what you don't.

Better to want what you get than get what you want.

Anyway, I think the point is... Pray. Meditate. Be grateful.

...

Yeah. yeah. yeah.

"All this sounds great, Doc. But what in the Sam Hill does it mean?"

I'm glad you asked.

Here is how you start to conquer your fear and crippling anxiety:

1. Look inside yourself and accept the present moment as it is. Understand that God has a plan for you, and his hand is guiding you.
2. Bring something good into the world. Take action that matters. It may not seem like much but it can grow.
3. Pray, Meditate, and Be Grateful for what is GOOD in your life. Give your worries to God ,by shaping them into thankfulness for the things you aren't worried about. And, maybe even thankful for the things you are worried about, because that's how you grow.

Rinse and repeat.

It's a practice. You don't wake up healed. You don't wake up enlightened. It takes work.

It takes faith, doubt, and perseverance.

I don't write for those that have their lives figured out. I write for those struggling to find inner peace.

Meditation
Spend 10-20 minutes shaping your anxiety into petitions and praises.

DAY 21

The Long View, the Struggle of the Will, and Becoming the Tide

I ran a marathon once.

It was horrible.

When I trained, I hurt.

By the time it got close to the race, I hurt every single day.

Knees, ankles, hips, back.

But you can't look back if you want to finish. You have to keep pushing forward. You have to know the difference between the pain that makes you stronger, and the pain that becomes an injury.

When training for something like this, your runs gradually become longer and longer. You struggle to push past your previous limit. Each week becomes more difficult than the next.

You might feel slower some days than others. You might have to take a week and run less in order for your body to recover. It takes months of grueling effort to train your body to run 26.2 miles. The people that are the best at this are the ones that keep the end game in mind (race day) while also getting lost in the present moment. They embrace the training but keep their eyes on the finish line.

If you ignore the training and only focus on the race, you will not be ready. If you ignore the race, then you will have no goal and will lose your reason for enduring such pain.

I call this The Long View.

It's the philosophy of seeing the big picture and the present moment as a whole. You're accepting what's happening now combined with preparing for tomorrow. Maybe tomorrow never comes. Maybe now is difficult and overwhelming. But, by placing the two side by side, you free yourself to follow a rambling path with as much control as fate allows.

It's like this: You want to be sober for 10 years. Well, in that case, it would be best to start today.

Okay, that was too obvious.

How about this: You worry about money. You probably think that you would have no stress or worries if you were rich. Well, maybe you can't get rich, but maybe you could be debt free. And, to be debt free in 5 years, you'd better start today with a budget and a plan.

These examples are just to show you a couple of obvious and practical ways this idea is applied.

But it's not really about preparation or planning at all. The connecting theme is not training or budgeting or being sober. The point is.... it takes ACTION. Action in the face of uncertainty. Action in the midst of pain.

You must act today, if you want any chance of building tomorrow.

Make no mistake, death is merely a breath away. But even in our death, we can celebrate life. We can be reborn to a future not yet dreamed of.

This is the Long View. A mindset and a dance. It's a dance between living in the NOW and accepting tomorrow's fate. And, taking action in the world that you control.

The thirst of life is too easily quenched by some. And at a moment's notice, they give in to the least resistance. Sometimes it feels easier to let the undertow pull you down, than it is to kick.

Do not seek refuge in the waves, safety on the beach, or stillness under the moon, but only... to become the tide.

The optimist can only know life, if he also knows death. You must die, in order to be reborn.

Nietzsche said it this way:

"To live is to suffer, to survive is to find some meaning in the suffering."

Struggle is a bitter concept, but one we must embrace. It is as much a part of us as we are of it. Our will to live is our answer to the struggle.

Optimism knows that struggle is part of the journey. It's inevitable. But we won't be stopped.

We keep pushing forward no matter the resistance.

The race is won by those that run.

Those part of the struggle, not separate.

Meditation

"Do you see what this means--all these pioneers who blazed the way, all these veterans cheering us on? It means we'd better get on with it. Strip down, start running--and never quit! No extra spiritual fat, no parasitic sins. Keep your eyes on Jesus, who both began and finished this race we're in. Study how he did it. Because he never lost sight of where he was headed--that exhilarating finish in and with God--he could put up with anything along the way: Cross, shame, whatever. And now he's there, in the place of honor, right alongside God. When you find yourselves flagging in your faith, go over that story again, item by item, that long litany of hostility he plowed through. That will shoot adrenaline into your souls!"

--Hebrews 12:1-3

Spend 10-20 minutes focused on your breathing.

DAY 22

Self Help Gurus are WORTHLESS!

"You can't keep your true self hidden forever; before long you'll be exposed. You can't hide behind a religious mask forever; sooner or later the mask will slip and your true face will be known."
--Luke 12: 2-3

Psychologist and author, Dr. Jordan Peterson said that life isn't made of matter. It's made of what matters.

In other words, the meaning of life, is the meaning.

I once had a patient ask me how she could discover purpose in life. But that's an unfair question. Because part of your purpose in life is discovering your purpose.

And I know this seems like circular logic. But let me explain.

You are more than one thing.

You are a combination of your principles and your actions. Your thoughts and your emotions. Your desires and your values. Your suffering and your growth.

It is impossible to separate out the parts. And if they don't match up....you will feel lost.

But the hero's journey has to start somewhere.

And the further the hero has to travel, the more desperate the plea of the innocent, the larger the dragon to be killed....the greater the story.

What does all this mean? It means, your purpose starts in your mind but then must be carried out into the physical world.

You "feel" how you tell your mind to feel. And you do what you tell your body to do.

Create your life with your actions, not your reactions.

Unhappy with your job? Find a new one.

Need more money? Sell everything you don't need and work your tail off.

Overweight? Get into the gym and stop eating crap food.

Tired of DHS in your business? Stop doing drugs, get a job, and act like you care.

Addicted to drugs? Minimize your possessions, start meditating, do something good for someone else, find a physician or mentor.

We all choose freedom. Freedom to choose. Freedom to fail. Freedom to be who we are. And in this freedom comes the complexities of anxiety, depression, addiction, disease, death, and heartbreak.

But that's how it has to be. You can't have the Yin without the Yang.

Where you're at now is not where you will always be.

Get your mind right. Start taking some right actions. And watch your life improve.

It may not be easy, but it's just that simple.

And this is just the beginning.

Okay, I kind of got side-tracked for a minute. This was supposed to be about finding your purpose.

So here it is...

Want to know your purpose?

You don't need self help.

You don't need a mastermind class.

You don't need "anointed prayer cloth".

You don't need to hide behind a mask.

You don't need a guru.

You don't need fake religion.

All you need is for God to shine a light so bright, that you will forever be changed.

<u>Meditation</u>
20 minutes in meditation, repeating this prayer: God, may your light shine. In me, in men, for all eternity, amen.

"Everything, a horse, a vine, is created for some duty. For what task, then, were you yourself created? A man's true delight is to do the things he was made for."
--Marcus Aurelius

DAY 23

What I should've said...

"Death and life are in the power of the tongue."
--Proverbs 18:21

She tells me treatment doesn't work.

She tells me therapy doesn't work.

She tells me she will never have a day that she doesn't want to use drugs.

I tell her to keep fighting.

I want to tell her that hopelessness is the same thing as death. It's a hell of your own making. But I don't think she's ready to hear that yet.

She asks me if it depresses me. This work I do. Hearing other people complain all day. Watching addicts struggle. I tell her no. I tell her I've seen people get through this, and I believe she will as well.

She doesn't believe me.

Words are powerful.

God speaks and the world is created.

With truth comes freedom.

The words we tell others and the words we tell ourselves. They matter.

I know the words that she needs to hear exist. They are out there floating around in the cosmos, just waiting to be found.

The combination of consonants and vowels that would make up the sentences that could change her life. The right words in the right order. Like a magic spell. And if I said these words, things would be better. But I don't know what those words are. I rarely do.

So, all I can really do is listen.

Because her words matter. Probably more than mine.

Her story is my story. And it's your story.

So I listen.

And I hope.

Hope she comes back next time.

Whether I have the words or not.

Prayer
God, give me the right words. Because there are people that need to hear them.

God, give me the time to listen. Because we're all in this thing together.

DAY 24

Don't iF Your Life Away

The disciples said to Jesus: "Tell us whom the kingdom of heaven is like!" He said to them: "It is like a mustard seed. It is the smallest of all seeds. But when it falls on cultivated soil, it produces a large branch and becomes shelter for the birds of the sky."

I've been in a really good mood lately.

I'm not sure why, but my serotonin levels must be off the chart.

And let me just be honest. I don't have any major stressors in my life right now.

The question you have to ask yourself is this: Does this make me unqualified to talk about how to overcome difficult circumstances?

But the next question you must ask is this: Am I just lucky? Or is it something else?

I'm knocking on wood here, because I know death and destruction are always around the corner. It waits for us all. I'm not talking about how to escape these things.

I'm talking about how to deal with life when you aren't getting what you hoped for. When it's not all rainbows and roses and unicorn noses.

Let me tell you one of the most dangerous words in the English language.

IF

What makes this word so destructive?

Because most people use it this way:

- I could get a better job...if I had a college degree
- I could be happy....if I just had another $1K a month
- I would be friendlier....if they were friendlier to me
- I would be successful....if everyone else would just do what I say
- I would be generous...if I just had a little more money
- I could lose weight...if my wife would stop cooking so much

You get the idea.

IF takes away your responsibility. It hides you behind excuses. It suffocates your self control. But most of all... it strangles your faith. Because you start to see life as something owed to you. Instead of seeing it as a gift.

What are you struggling with?

Money?

Love?

Family?

Job?

Now, think about how you're using the word **IF**. And turn it around.

DON'T iF YOUR LIFE AWAY

What do you have control over? Accept these things and leave the rest in the dust.

Jesus said you've got to know what's in front of you first, then the things that are hidden will be seen.

In other words, you've got to come face to face with reality and make a decision. Will you do your part? Or, will you allow the worries of the world to choke out your destiny?

The world is full of possibilities. The world is abundant. Your life can be anything you make it.

You can have purpose and meaning. Or, you can choose to be miserable.

The choice is yours!

But maybe your circumstances are blocking you from seeing the big picture. Maybe you're too sick to believe you can be healthy. Maybe you're too addicted to believe you can be free. Maybe things just seem too difficult. Good times seem too far away.

Well, that's what I'm here for. To show you a better way. A new way to look.

So what if you're walking around blind......because I know the guy giving out free glasses.

The first thing you've got to do is get **IF** out of your vocabulary. Because you can't be happy if'ing your life away.

Here's the truth: Your circumstances don't matter. I mean, of course they matter. But they don't decide your destiny. That's my point. I don't have a magic wand to take away all the pain in your life. I do, however, h,ave a magic wand to help you accept the situation you are in and RISE ABOVE.

IF

It has potential for great things. But if you're not careful, it will crush you where you stand.

So be cautious.

Be positive.

Be confident.

Be good.

Or at least.....

act as IF you are.

<u>Meditation</u>
Time to actually show a little faith.   Not faith over circumstances. But faith through circumstances.

Spend 10 to 20 minutes in prayer and meditation.

DAY 25

IKIGAI

IKIGAI

It's a Japanese term. It means reason for living. Purpose. Your meaning. What drives you. Etc.

People like to ask me about time management. How do I fit it all in? Wife, 5 kids, 4 businesses, daily exercise, writing, lunch with friends. It all gets done. And I don't feel stretched too thin.

The answer is: Ikigai. I follow my purpose.

I do the things I love, and I try to limit the rest. It's the 80/20 rule. 20% of the stuff you do brings about 80% of the results you want. So, I built my life around the 20%.

I don't "manage" my time. I fill my time with the things that I enjoy.

I treat a lot of people that struggle with anxiety, depression, and sometimes addiction. They often feel their life is meaningless. Or, that it's spinning out of control. They see no purpose. No point. They can't see past their pain.

No matter how far you've fallen or how bad things seem to be, please understand this: Your life still has meaning.

The beauty of life is in it's regeneration. As long as you're alive, there's time. Resurrection can happen with the non-dead as well.

Stop doing the things you hate and start doing things that have meaning. This doesn't mean you have to save the world. That job has already been done. Focus on small things. Let the small things build over time. And then watch your life overflow.

There's a difference between happiness and meaning. Find happiness in small things. Just don't focus too much on happiness. Instead focus on meaning.

There is a world out there for you to discover. And you don't even have to leave home to find it. The adventure starts inside. A map of meaning. A treasure of indescribable worth.

You were created in the image of God. Now believe it.

There is purpose inside of you. And when you start to pursue your true life, the pull of drugs will be lessened. Anxiety will be lifted. Despair will be crushed. And your life will be yours again.

Maybe not at first. But with time.

We all know people that have completely thrown away their life. We think..."What a shame."

But, what is it we think they have done wrong? Why is it sad to see this?

Because life has meaning.

So find yours.

Meditation

"Knowing what is right is like deep water in the heart;

a wise person draws from the well within."
--Proverbs 20:5

Spend 10 to 20 minutes focused on your breathing.

DAY 26

I've Come to Start a Fire on this Earth

"I've come to start a fire on this earth. How I wish it were blazing right now!"
--Luke 12:49

I knew a guy once. He hated people. He hated God. He hated himself.

He tried to commit suicide.

He struggled with drugs.

He struggled with living.

He couldn't see anything good as possible in his life. It was beyond his imagination.

There is nothing worse than living a life without passion. Without joy. Without the WILL to live.

Jesus offers us this.

And before you start shaking your head or rolling your eyes. You need to understand that it doesn't matter what your science books say, or what your history books teach. Truth is truth.

And you can't find purpose from your idea of facts.

This is actually a problem with mainstream Christianity. They often think that belief has something to do with historical knowledge and acceptance of facts.

NOPE!

Belief is something different. Belief is something powerful and mysterious.

Faith is a fire, burning inside you.

It burns your walls down.

It leaves you raw.

And, in this unprotected state, you can finally see yourself for who you are. What you are. And what you are becoming.

God wills you into existence with his breath. And leaves most of the rest up to you.

What we see in this life. The good and the bad. It's our responsibility.

Our prayers must become our actions.

Our rescue must be self absorbed and then self released.

We look into the abyss and stare with cold dark eyes, hardened hands, and focused minds.

We are ready.

We will overcome.

Meditation

20 minute walking meditation. Repeat the mantra "I am abundance in action".

DAY 27

THE PLANS

"I know the plans I have for you. Plans to
prosper. Plans for hope."
--Jeremiah 29:11

When I was younger, I wanted to know what my purpose was. I
wanted a clear path to follow. I felt if I didn't know, then I would be
lost.

But later, I came to understand that the path is not clear, it is
cleared.

Your purpose is the path

There is an idea in the Bible that God has plans for us. Plans for big
things. But, it's our choice if we decide to follow along or go our
own way.

A lot of people read this verse and think that it means their lives
should be easy and without pain. Well, that's a lie. No life has ever
been easy and without pain. Suffering is essential to life. We all
die. There is no escape.

"Don't run from suffering; embrace it. Follow me
and I'll show you how. Self-help is no help at all.
Self-sacrifice is the way, my way, to finding
yourself, your true self. What kind of deal is it to
get everything you want but lose yourself? What
could you ever trade your soul for?"
--Matthew 10: 24-26

God offers something more than a life of suffering or a life of prosperity. He offers us a life of meaning.

You see, free will is a tricky thing. You can't have the benefit of free will in your life without dealing with other people's free will in your life.

In other words: you are free to choose good, but your neighbor is free to choose evil.

If God's plan was for us to be robots, then that's what we'd be. But, instead his plan for us is something else.

His plan for us....is our potential.

To meet our full potential. To meet at the border of greatness and mystery and look deep into our consciousness and KNOW.

And with this potential comes responsibility.

We aren't in this life alone.

We are not islands.

We are the wind, the waves, and the ocean floor.

We are ONE.

And with this we must become something greater than even our potential can match.

We must give.

We must release from ourselves this very life force that carries us forward.

And by this great sacrifice.....

WE BECOME WHAT WE ARE
Meditation
Meditate for 5 minutes by repeating this mantra: <u>I follow. God leads. I have purpose. I have meaning. I am.</u>

DAY 28

THE WORD BECAME FLESH

"The word became flesh."
--John 1:4

I read a blog post one day. It was about Jesus. Written by a non-christian.

It was a good article. It wasn't sacrilegious. He wasn't making fun of anyone or questioning anyone's beliefs. I read the comments. It made my skin crawl.

You see, there were all these "christians" trying to convert the guy in the comments section.

I know they meant well. They were focused on his soul. Saving him. If they didn't use this opportunity to shove their beliefs down his throat, when else would they be able to?

I had to think, "Is this what we're like?"

Is that me?

But, I think it's really anyone that believes something.

Think about a movie that you loved. When it was over, you wanted to tell someone about it. You wanted to share with them the experience. And think about how fun it is to tell someone about a book or movie, and they've already seen it or read it and felt the same way as you. Your brain makes a pleasant connection.

But is that the same thing?

When was the last time you told someone that if they didn't watch Star Wars, they would surely burn in hell for eternity. Or, that if they didn't read Lord of the Rings, their life would have no meaning. (Okay, I'll admit that was unfair because if you don't watch Star Wars or read Lord of the Rings then I question the safety of your soul as well.)

Back to the point...

Our experiences and beliefs are important. But, we aren't just meant to tell a story, spread, a message, or give a warning. We are meant to live a message. We are meant to bring good news to the poor, the imprisoned, the depressed.

And words alone will never do the job.

Because true hope can only be born on the wings of life.

I'm afraid many Christians are only looking to the skies for God to come down and make things right. Heal the disease. Cure the heartache. Put the sinners to shame.

But those folks missed an important piece of history. Because that already happened. And now we are what's left. To bring hope to the hopeless. We are God's will, on earth as it is in heaven.

God works through us. We are not only his voice. We are his hands and feet.

Our lives are the message.

Our message is our meaning.

Our hearts the true story.

Our intent means nothing.

It is our actions that matter.

I remember treating a little girl in Nicaragua. She was probably 4 or 5 years old. She had a fluffy green dress. She had dressed in her best clothes to walk 3 hours to the dirty tin roof clinic. I gave her penicillin for an infected ear.

It didn't seem like much to me.

A few years later, I'm talking to another doctor. He didn't understand what good it does to go overseas and treat people for a week. He said they'd just be sick again and without help as soon as you left the country.

He wasn't heartless. Just practical.

I told him that if I go this week, and someone else goes next week, then they wouldn't be without help. But this takes faith. And it takes me being willing to do my part for at least one small week, even if no one else does.

But what I should have told him was this...

The finger is pointing at the moon.

Stop looking at the finger.

Look at the moon.

<u>Meditation</u>

Meditate for 10 to 20 minutes. Focus on the message that your life is spreading. Take control of what you can control and take your life in the direction you want it to go.

DAY 29

HOW TO KILL A GIANT

Five smooth stones. But all he needed was one.

After the Giant was dead, David took the sword and took his head.
Not all stories end this way. Not every battle will seem as easy. Not
every Giant will fall as hard.

So, how do you kill a giant?

1) Start with courage

It is interesting how often the Bible teaches us "Fear Not".

Fear is a normal emotion. Anxiety is a natural phenomenon. But far
too often we begin to feel overwhelmed, and this state of fear
becomes our baseline. We look for comfort in the familiar. Afraid
to take action.

God is constantly calling us back. Giving us comfort. Teaching us
to be brave and trust in Him.

> "The Lord is my Light and Salvation. With him by my side, I am
> fearless. Afraid of no one and no thing."
> --Psalm 27:1 (my interpretation)

Courage isn't the lack of fear, but doing the right thing in spite of
your fears.

It's standing up to giants even when you're facing death.

2) Have faith

What you believe about life is how life will be. Your mind creates
your reality. This doesn't mean that there aren't real things that cause
you pain and hardship. It doesn't mean that it's all in your head.

What this means is how you respond to the bad things that happen to
you is what determines if you make it through or not.

And this takes faith. Because sometimes God feels close, and
sometimes God feels distant. But, our faith in His presence and
goodness is what guides us. It's our faith that God is Love. (1 John
4:7-8)

It starts with simple faith that God will guide us. Expect the best.
Do not settle! And pray...often.

When times are difficult, when you're facing pain, when you think
all is lost.....Believe!

Faith is a strange thing. One minute you think it's pointless and in a
moment... your whole life can change.

3) Take action

There's an old Chinese proverb "Better to be a warrior in a garden than a gardener in a war".

Life comes at you, so be prepared.

We can't escape death. We can't escape pain. We can't escape suffering.

But, we can meet our trials head on. We can face the giant with whatever weapons we have available.

In other words, we're all going to die. The least we can do is go down throwing rocks. And who knows? Maybe we live to fight another day.

David had the courage to stand for what was right and meet the giant in the battlefield. He had the courage to let the bastard know his time had come.

He had faith in his God and a hand full of pebbles.

And the giant came crashing down.

Meditation

"Who is this uncircumcised Philistine, that he should defy the armies of the living God?"

--1 Samuel 17:26

Spend 20 minutes and focus on God's presence. Imagine it encapsulating you and giving you courage and strength. As you breathe, you breathe it in. As you breathe out, it surrounds you and guards you.

DAY 30

The Cross

"Maybe self improvement isn't the answer.
Maybe self destruction is the answer."
--Fight Club

Jesus died on a cross.

A Roman execution.

The cross: the iconic symbol of Christianity. Constructed for torture. Built to kill. But what was meant as damnation has become the crux of salvation.

I've heard people criticize Christians for their use of the cross as a picture of faith. "It's like wearing an electric chair around your neck." But Christians have this strange belief that the end is not the end. And this symbol of death is really just a reminder of the power of God over death.

Jesus put it this way:

"You don't have to wait for the End. I am, right now, Resurrection and Life. The one who believes in me, even though he or she dies, will live. And everyone who lives believing in me does not ultimately die at all. Do you believe this?"
--John 11:25-26

Life isn't all rainbows and unicorns. Life is cancer, betrayal, addiction, flat tires, bounced checks, and broken bones. Life is a cross.

Jesus said, "Pick up your cross and follow me."

We are given a choice. Allow the cross to crush us or pick it up and follow the path.

The WILL is what drives us. The will to live. The will to push forward. The will to become.

We die to ourselves to truly know ourselves. Our pride and ego cast aside. We dive into the depths of Hell and emerge something else altogether. We are born again.

Sometimes it takes death to see life. Pain to see joy. Misery to find happiness.

Purpose above all and through all.

It has become "foolish" to believe in life after death. To believe in mystery is madness. To have faith is a mental disorder. But what if there was more to it than this?

Imagine with me the universe. There is more undiscovered than discovered. More unexplored than seen. What part of us closes our minds to the possibility of something else? Something unexplainable? Something hidden but beautiful.

Of course Jesus taught that the kingdom of heaven was in our midst. Was he talking about himself? Or was he telling us to stop wasting our lives?

It's easy to throw your hands up and tell yourself that this life doesn't matter. You'll be in heaven some day, and your problems will be over. But if you waste this life, what's to keep you from wasting the next life?

Don't miss out on what's in front of you. Don't look to the skies. Don't look to the future. Look inside yourself. Allow God to move in your life TODAY. There are people that are hurting. There are people living in a world of pain. You can help them.

All of our material world will rust, rot, and die.

Too many people are sitting around just waiting for the world to end. Forget that.

Pick up you cross. And become who you are...who God designed you to be.

Now watch the spirit throw mountains into the sea.

Meditation
"We despised him and rejected him;
he endured suffering and pain.
No one would even look at him--
we ignored him as if he were nothing.
"But he endured the suffering that should have been ours,
the pain that we should have borne.
All the while we thought that his suffering
was punishment sent by God.
But because of our sins he was wounded,
beaten because of the evil we did.
We are healed by the punishment he suffered,
made whole by the blows he received."
--Isaiah 53:5-6
20 minutes focused on God's redemptive power.

Alright guys and gals. There you have it. 30 days of devotions. Written by me. A nobody.

Feel free to crack open that Bible and brain of yours, think it through, and question everything I wrote.

But just remember....all the reading, writing, thinking, prophesying, singing, and shouting.....don't mean a thing if you ain't got love.

Be weird.

Be kind.

Be you.

P.S.

Thanks for reading

Dr Chris Park is a family physician and addiction doctor living and working in the hills of Mississippi. Husband, father, brutal optimist.

You can find out more at his website:

doctorchrispark.com

Made in the USA
Las Vegas, NV
22 January 2021